Alison Pohn is a well-known writer of children's books. She was a little concerned to find herself suddenly writing for an older crowd, but then she looked in the mirror. She lives in Chicago with her husband, her daughter, and three cats. She takes good care of her teeth and is expecting a prescription for bifocals at her next optometrist's appointment.

Additional Contributing Writers: Emily Thornton Calvo, Erika Cornstuble, and Paul Seaburn

Louis Weber, CEO
Publications International, Ltd.
7373 North Cicero Avenue
Lincolnwood, Illinois 60712

Permission is never granted for commercial purposes.

ISBN-13: 978-1-4127-1364-1
ISBN-10: 1-4127-1364-1

Manufactured in China.

8 7 6 5 4 3 2 1

Laugh Lines

Getting Old Is Funny!

Written by Alison Pohn

Publications International, Ltd.

Stanley, I'll bet you two tokens that they've gotten smaller stools since we were here last.

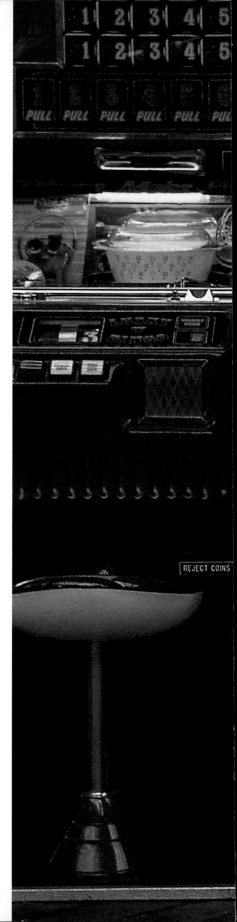

Ed's toothless smile turned to a frown when he realized his wife had said "steaks," not "shakes," for dinner.

Here's a tip:

T-shirt on.

Chin up.

Earl could never figure out why Lena was always so refreshed after an afternoon of errands in town.

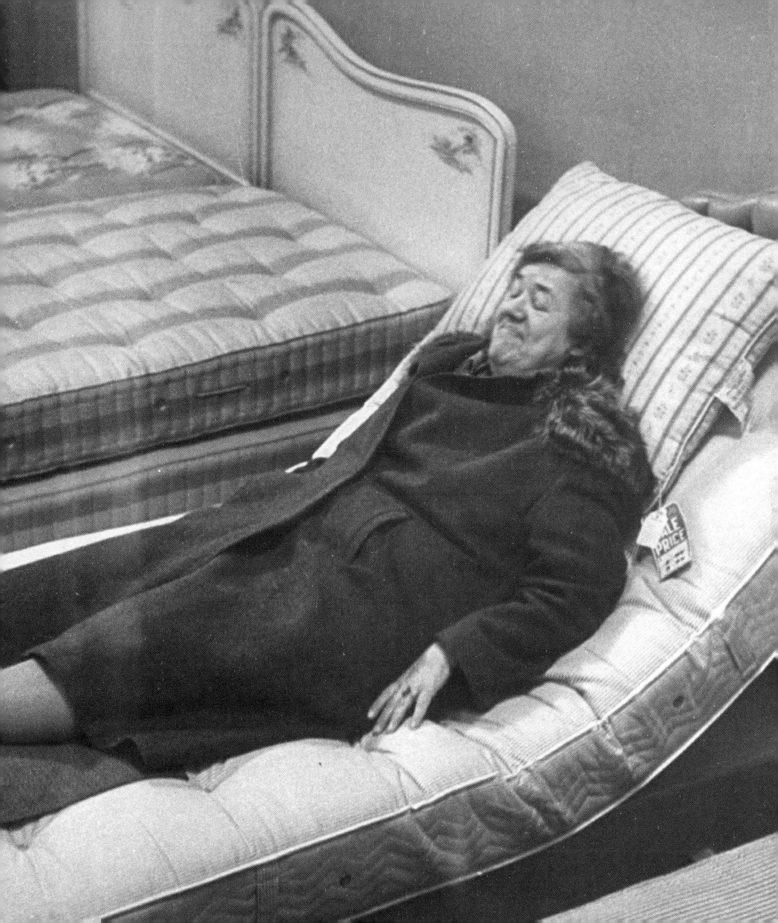

Sure, it wasn't the Chippendales,
but the women of Shady Springs
Retirement Home appreciated the effort.

Mary-Kate and Ashley,

consider this a warning.

Myra wondered if she should reconsider the issue of hormone replacement therapy.

Oh, sure. You're
fooling everyone.

By her 13th grandchild,

Ida had become pretty laid back.

Men. Who needs 'em?

Being beautiful is hard work.

—Eleanor, how did you get

those shapely thighs?

—Why, walking 10 miles

to and from school,

uphill both ways,

you silly girl.

I've got those sliding dentures,

can't see without my glasses,

I hate gravity blues.

Oh, great. This means my husband's at home walking a fried chicken.

34

I think Grandpa has a squirrel in his ear!

"Be good and you
will be lonesome."

—Mark Twain

Careful, Marshall, or you'll end up
with both sets of teeth.

My body's a temple—the temple of doom.

The girls liked to park it right outside Starbucks and taunt the clients with real, percolated coffee.

Remember when your
daily workout was more than
just tying your shoes?

Margie realized—albeit too late—

where little Mary had hidden her oatmeal.

Helen and Marian slept on,
secure in the knowledge that
no one else on the bus
remembered where they
were going either.

Cute babe.

Awesome blue rinse.

Don't look. Okay, quick, look!

Fifty-two Christmases,

fifty-two housedresses.

Are you sure this is the right fountain? I'm not feeling any younger.

Take the picture already.
We're wrinkling like
prunes in here.

Don't mind me.
I'm just sitting here
working out my
retirement plan.

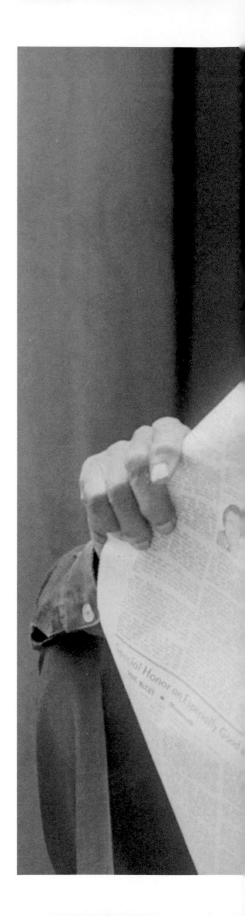

I'm sorry, what was

your name again?

Kings of the
Wild Frontier, indeed.

Oh no, sir. We don't want to buy insurance. We just wanted some company.

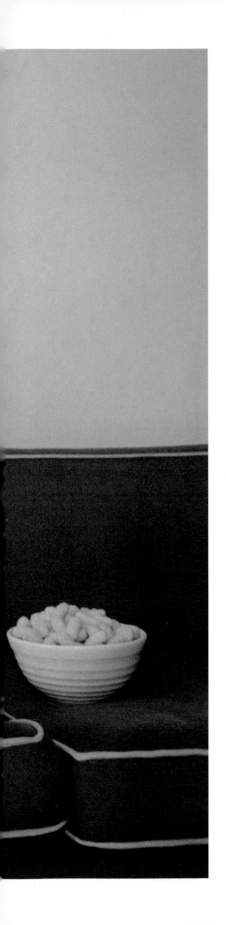

Stayin' alive!

Stayin' alive!

Beauty really is skin-deep.

This one . . .

This one's about the

size of my prostate.

Why, I believe this gum is

older than we are!

Girls still wanna
have fun.

Who needs a helmet when you know

how to use hair spray?

You're right—the curlers DO give you better reception.

I got prescription drug coverage!

I got prescription drug coverage!

My fastball was clocked in the mid-70s.

No, wait ... that was me!

These are nothing. I carried a 200-pound dumbbell for 30 years ... then I left him.

Don't laugh! I get incredible mileage.

Forget the tour bus—let's stay here and watch those hunks clean the pool.

We always suspected Phyllis and
Fifi had the same hairdresser.

Get me to that yard sale—pronto!

He followed me home. Can I keep him?